MILLIONS OF CARS
From Drawing Board to Highway

MILLIONS OF CARS
From Drawing Board
to Highway

by **Hal Butler**
Illustrated with photographs

Julian Messner New York

BOOKS BY HAL BUTLER

MILLIONS OF CARS
   From Drawing Board to Highway

BASEBALL ALL-STAR GAME THRILLS

THE BOB ALLISON STORY

THE HARMON KILLEBREW STORY

ROAR OF THE ROAD
   The Story of Auto Racing

STORMIN' NORMAN CASH

THERE'S NOTHING NEW IN SPORTS
   The Story of How Sports Began

UNDERDOGS OF SPORT

THE WILLIE HORTON STORY

Published by Julian Messner, a Division of Simon & Schuster, Inc.
1 West 39 Street, New York, N.Y. 10018. All rights reserved.

Printed in the United States of America
ISBN 0-671-32508-6 Cloth Trade
ISBN 0-671-32509-4 MCE

Library of Congress Catalog Card No. 74-180531

Designed by Virginia M. Soulé

Acknowledgments

A note of thanks to two librarians—Elizabeth T. Fast, Director of Library Services, Groton (Connecticut) Public Schools, and Lore Howard, Chief, Bureau of School Libraries, New York State Department of Education—who first sparked the idea for this book. Also, a bow of gratitude to those at Ford Motor Company who aided in the book's preparation—Theodore H. Mecke, Jr., Walter T. Murphy, John E. Sattler, Roland W. Williams, Richard Ruddell, George Haviland, Bill Goodell, Milt West, Marty Garter, Rudy Fischer, Joe Kogl, and Fred Thompson. But above all, a big thank-you to Lee A. Iacocca, President of Ford Motor Company. Had he not "fathered" the Mustang, I could not have "fathered" this book.

A Note to the Reader

To tell the story of how a car is born, I have chosen to write about the Mustang. It was the first sporty, rally-type car ever produced by an American auto maker, and the rapid rate at which it was built and sold is a good example of modern mass production.

Today, American cars of this kind are popular. You see them on the road wherever you go. But before 1964, there were no such cars. In that year, Ford Motor Company introduced the Mustang. In two years, there were a million Mustangs on the road. Soon other American automobile manufacturers produced similar types of cars.

Contents

Why The Mustang?

Planning a new car is a risky business. It costs millions of dollars, and it may take as long as three years to produce an automobile. Sometimes the new car is a success. Sometimes it is a failure. To make the new car a success, the manufacturer must plan it right and build it right. People must want to buy it more than any other new car.

What made the Mustang such a big success? Why did it sell faster than other cars? Did Ford just *happen* to come up with the right car at the right time? Was Ford simply lucky?

Not at all. Ford officials—led by Lee A. Iacocca, often called "the father of the Mustang"—knew several years before the Mustang was built that people were ready to buy a sleek, sporty-type car.

It all started in November, 1960, when Ford asked its Marketing Research Department to find out just what kind of car the American public wanted. The best

In April of 1968, the two-millionth Mustang rolled off the line. Lee Iacocca, the "father of the Mustang," is shown standing beside the driver.

way to find out was to ask. Marketing Research did just that.

Hundreds of men and women were interviewed by phone and at their homes. They were asked such questions as: "What kind of a car do you want to buy next time? Which of these two sketches of future cars do you like best? What colors do you prefer? What styling do you like? Do you like a sporty-looking car? Do you like bucket seats? Do you want an economical car?"

When all the questions were answered, these facts became known: (1) millions of young people would become car buyers in the 1960s; (2) almost all of them liked the sports car look; (3) many families were anxious to buy a second car, and they wanted their second car to be small and economical.

So Ford had its answers. The new car had to be a sports car type. It had to perform well and look good. And it had to be priced low.

How do you build such a car? Ford officials were not at all sure it could be done. But they knew there was no such car on the market. And they were sure that if they built one, people would buy it.

So they decided to try.

Planning And Styling

Turning a dream car into a real one is a big job. It begins with the work done by a department called Product Planning. This department is the bridge between the company and the customer. Members of this department study what the customer wants. Then they come up with a "paper plan" which includes all the specifications (details and measurements) for the new car—everything except what it will look like and what it will be called.

In the case of Ford's new sporty-type car (not yet named Mustang), they decided the car could be no more than 180 inches long. It could weigh no more than 2,500 pounds. It had to seat four passengers. It had to sell for a low price.

Product planners, stylists and engineers work on a "paper plan" which precedes the actual styling and assembly of a car.

These were the major goals that had to be met.

The next step was to design the car. This is the job of a group of artists called designers. These men began sketching their ideas of what the new car should look like. They sketched hundreds of ideas. Some sketches were of the complete car. Others were of the interior only.

The best sketches were made into larger illustrations with more details added. These drawings, or renderings, were studied again to see which came closest to the kind of car Ford wanted.

Once it was decided what the car should look like, the renderings were given to two groups of skilled

An automobile is designed around the driver and passengers. Two-dimensional mannequins called "Oscars" are used to figure out dimensions for head room, knee room, leg room, and head-to-windshield clearance. These engineers are "proving out" a new design.

The drawing board is one of the first steps in creating a car. Skilled stylists make hundreds of sketches before clay models are made.

The interior designer works on interior parts such as instrument panels, air conditioning outlets, steering wheels, radio speakers and other such items.

sculptors. One group built full-size wood models of the car's interior. Actual paint and fabrics were used to make the interior of the car look exactly as it would when it was produced.

The second group of sculptors started making two mock-ups—full-size clay models of the cars. Making mock-ups is always an interesting job, but this time it was exciting! One of the mock-ups was to be the start of an entirely different type of automobile!

In producing a full-size clay model, a rough frame is first made of wood. This frame, or arma-

The earliest step in clay modeling—the placing of clay over the wood framework or armature.

ture, is the general shape of the new car. The sculptors then add clay to the framework and smooth it down to the exact shape they want. Sometimes they use as much as 6,000 pounds of clay in making the full-size model!

The clay model is dressed up with decal-like paper called Di-noc. Colored paper is used for the body. Dark paper is used for the windows. Alumi-

A full-size clay model of the Mustang takes shape under the skillful hands of these sculptors.

num foil takes the place of chrome moldings, bumpers, and door handles. Even lettering is added.

When the mock-up is finished, it is such a perfect job that it looks just like a car made of steel!

Finally the designers were ready to show the two clay models to Ford officials. They hoped the "bosses" would approve one of the models so that the new car could go into production. The officials liked the general idea of the car, but they did not approve either model.

The designers were disappointed. They went back to their drawing boards and piles of clay to try again.

Producing the new car had now become a race against time. It was December, 1961. Mr. Iacocca wanted to introduce the new car in the spring of 1964. To meet this deadline, it would be necessary to have an approved clay model by the summer of 1962.

That meant plenty of work. Between December, 1961, and July, 1962, designers turned out eighteen clay models. One of them was a racy car with a long hood and short rear deck (trunk area) that caught the eye of Ford officials. But they weren't quite satisfied, and they asked that more work be done on it.

This clay modeler has just applied Di-noc, a decal-like paper, to a clay model to indicate window glass.

Time was critical, so a "crash" program was started. Two crews of sculptors worked day and night for two weeks to come up with a "winner." Developing a clay model in two weeks was unheard of in the auto industry, but the two crews produced seven of them!

The officials again examined the models. One sleek model stood out above all others. Henry Ford II kept going back to it. So did Mr. Iacocca.

"This is what you want to do?" Mr. Ford asked.

This is the clay model of the Mustang that was approved by Ford officials on August 16, 1962. This car, with almost no changes, finally rolled off the final assembly line on March 9, 1964.

"Yes," said Mr. Iacocca, "that's the car we should build."

"Okay," said Mr. Ford. "Let's go with it."

The decision had been made. The new car would be built. But what would they call it? It was decided that the name had to be two syllables long—and exciting. They tried everything from Aardvark to Zebra.

Finally they decided to call the car Mustang. The reason? Because Mustang is described as "small, hardy and half wild." What better name could there be for a sassy-looking car?

All Ford had to do now was produce the car. But that was a big job. Normally it would take two to three years to produce. This time, however, it had to be ready by early March, 1964!

They only had eighteen months!

The galloping mustang which is the emblem on all Mustang cars was created by Waino Kangas, a skilled clay sculptor for nearly twenty years.

The Torture Tests

Before any car goes into production, hand-built models called prototypes are made for testing. Testing these prototypes to make sure they perform right is the job of the engineers.

A hand-built prototype may cost as much as $150,000 to make. You would think such a valuable car would be treated with great care. But that isn't so. The engineers actually *mistreat* it to find out how long it will hold up under severe punishment.

"We treat the cars rough," says one engineer. "In about two months we give a car the same punishment a customer gives it in 80,000 miles of driving." This is done by a series of "torture tests" on the test track and in the laboratories.

In late 1962 and early 1963, prototypes of the new Mustang were tested. The engineers drove them at high speeds for long periods of time around the test track. They took them over jarring cobblestone roads, over deep chuckholes, and up and down curbs. They rattled the cars over "washboard" roads. They ran them through a ditch filled with water to see if body leaks developed. They checked the steering, the acceleration, and the braking.

Meanwhile, in the laboratory, engineers tested the individual parts of the car under conditions much

The cobblestones—a famous bit of torture that tests all undercarriage parts. A ride over these cobblestones shakes the car unmercifully.

more severe than normal driving. Springs, for example, were put under severe pressure, hour after hour, until they broke. If they broke too soon, the parts were redesigned to make them stronger. Other parts were tested in the same way.

But even that wasn't all. In designing the Mustang, safety engineers had to be sure that the car was as safe to drive as possible. Long before the Mustang was built, these special engineers had been working hard to make all cars safer.

How did they go about this? Mainly, by de-

The curb test checks out wheel balance and tires.

stroying hundreds of cars in deliberate crashes. Cars were crashed head-on. They were sideswiped. They were smashed against barriers. They were rolled over.

In these automobiles were life-like dummies, resembling the human body in weight and construction. Sensitive electronic instruments were placed in the dummies which described their movements inside the car at the time of a crash. High-speed cameras also took movies of the crashes.

Studying these crashes enabled safety engineers to locate the major injury areas in a car's interior. The studies resulted in such safety features as seat belts, shoulder straps, padded instrument panels, steering wheels that collapsed on impact, seat anchors, and many others. Such devices now appear on all cars. And there will be more of them as safety engineers continue to study and create new safety features.

In the case of the Mustang, it was only after engineers were satisfied that every part of the new car was able to stand up under the worst a driver could give it—and that safety devices had been installed—that they released the car for production.

The Mustang would be manufactured at Ford's Rouge plant.

The Amazing Rouge Plant

Detroit, Michigan, is called the Motor City because the major automobile companies are located there. Ford's Rouge Plant is where the first Mustangs were built. It is located on the Rouge River in Dearborn, a suburb of Detroit, and is the largest manufacturing plant in the world.

Just to give you an idea how big the plant is: it covers 1,200 acres of ground; it generates enough electricity every day to light the homes of one million people; it burns enough coal daily to heat 330,000 homes; and it uses 425 million gallons of water every day!

But what makes the Rouge so remarkable is that it is the only *complete* auto-making plant in the world. It has everything necessary for manufacturing cars. It makes its own car bodies, engines, chassis, radiators, and other parts. It even has its own steel mill and a plant for making glass. And it has its own assembly plant where the cars are put together, piece by piece—just like a jigsaw puzzle!

An aerial view of the huge Rouge Plant with two ore freighters docked at the bins.

How Steel Is Made

The basic metal used in building cars is steel, and thousands of tons of steel are used every day at the Rouge Plant. Ford buys half of its steel from steel companies. But the other half it makes right at the plant.

How is steel made?

Iron ore, which looks like red-brown sand, is the major ingredient of steel. Ford gets its iron ore from the Mesabi Range in Minnesota. It is brought to the Rouge Plant in Ford's own ships. Huge cranes unload the freighters at dockside, dumping more than three million tons of ore into storage bins each year.

The ore, along with coke and limestone,

is fed into three blast furnaces. These huge furnaces are ten stories high! And temperatures in the furnaces reach 2,700 degrees Fahrenheit!

This basic oxygen furnace produces steel from molten iron and scrap steel. It produces 240 tons of molten steel in less than an hour.

These red-hot ribbons of steel were once cylinderical shaped ingots. When cooled, the ribbons will be rolled into coils and sent to the stamping plant for the manufacture of car body parts.

This great heat turns the mixture into red-hot molten iron. The iron is poured into torpedo-shaped railroad cars, which carry the iron to the basic oxygen furnace. This furnace mixes 200 tons of molten iron with 90 tons of scrap steel. Forty-five minutes later this mixture becomes high-grade steel.

This steel is then poured into cylinder-shaped molds which form ingots. The ingots weigh from five to sixteen tons each. They are taken to a reheating furnace, or soaking pit, where they are heated to temperatures that make them soft enough to shape easily. The ingots are then rolled into strips—just like dough flattened under a rolling pin. After the strips cool and harden, they are rolled up into coils that weigh 60,000 pounds each and are about a mile long. The coils are then sent to the stamping plant to be shaped into body parts by great presses.

How Glass Is Made

The Rouge glass plant makes glass for use in car windows and windshields.

The basic material for glass is silica sand. Sand is mixed with other material, including limestone, soda ash, and charcoal. The mixture is heated in a glass furnace at about 2,800 degrees Fahrenheit until it melts together. Then this mixture goes through what is called the float process.

In this process, a long ribbon of glass flows out of a furnace onto a flat molten tin surface. As the glass flows along, the heat is gradually reduced until the glass hardens.

In twenty-four hours, the Rouge glass plant produces a glass ribbon eleven miles long, one hundred inches wide, and one-eighth of an inch thick. This long ribbon is cut into smaller pieces for use in cars.

A continuous ribbon of finished glass flows at the rate of 30 feet per minute from the float facility at Rouge. As glass emerges, it is inspected and cut to desired lengths. This alignment conveyor guides the glass sheets through the cutters which trim the sheets into twin pieces to be used in the manufacture of laminated safety-glass windows.

Making Parts For Cars

Do you know how many parts there are in an automobile? A hundred? Two hundred? Wrong. There are more than 13,000 parts in a modern car! Everything from bolts and nuts to the side panels and the roofs of an automobile.

Two groups at the Rouge, the Foundry Operation and the Stamping Operation, produce car parts, each by a different method.

The Foundry Operation produces engine blocks, cylinder heads, camshafts, and similar parts. These parts are made by pouring molten metal into a mold to give it the shape desired. A part formed in this manner is called a casting. The rough casting is then further shaped and smoothed by machines. For example, the rough casting of an engine block goes through 600 separate operations to convert it into a six- or eight-cylinder engine.

The Stamping Operation uses the coils of steel shipped to them from the steel mill to make body parts. Huge stamping presses shape steel sheets or strips into car roofs, side panels, fenders, hoods, trunk lids and other such parts. These great presses have huge mouths into which the steel is fed. The lower jaw of the mouth is called the die; the upper part is called the punch. The two come together with a smashing sound to stamp the steel in the form needed.

Huge presses like this one stamp out body parts for today's cars.

Mass Production—And
The Final Assembly Line

The final assembly line in an automobile factory is an amazing sight. As the car moves slowly down the line, parts are added to it by workers standing along the line. One by one the body, the front fenders, the seats, the wheels —big pieces and small—are attached to the car. When the automobile reaches the end of the line, it is complete.

The final assembly line is the finest example of mass production.

What is mass production?

Simply stated, mass production is the manufacture of goods in large quantities. In other words, it is the ability to turn out millions of cars, refrigerators, television sets, and other merchandise quickly and at low cost.

If all merchandise were made by hand, one item at a time, it would take more time and cost more when you bought it. Remember the hand-made prototype car that cost $150,000 to build? If that was the way all cars had to be built, few people would be able to own a car.

A view of the final assembly line as the first 1965 Mustangs were put together.

With mass production, though, merchandise of all kinds can be built quickly and in great numbers, and the cost to produce each piece of merchandise is less. Therefore, each piece of merchandise can be sold at a lower price. More people can buy the things they need and want. Not only that, but producing things in quantity makes more jobs for more people. And because more people are working and earning money, they can buy the things that make their lives more comfortable.

Many people believe that Henry Ford, who founded the Ford Motor Company, invented the moving assembly line. That isn't true. The idea was used one hundred years earlier in milling grain and manufacturing guns. But Henry Ford was the first man to use the system to produce automobiles.

Henry Ford was born in Springwells Township, near the Detroit suburb of Dearborn, Michigan, on July 30, 1863. Henry's father was a farmer, and he hoped his son would also be a farmer. But young Henry showed a keen interest in mechanics. In fact, he spent so much of his time in a small machine shop, puttering around, that he neglected his school work and his farm chores. By the time he was fifteen, he had built his first steam engine.

Henry left school when he was seventeen, and worked as a machinist's apprentice in several Detroit shops. In the winter of 1893, he became interested in internal combustion (gasoline) engines and built a small one-cylinder model. Later he constructed a larger engine and mounted it on a frame fitted with four bicycle wheels. This vehicle was called a quadricycle and was Henry Ford's first "automobile." He went on to found the Ford Motor Company in 1903, and the first car built by the company was sold on July 23 of that year.

At that time, cars were built just like houses—by hand as they stood in one place. The frame, or chassis, of the car would be placed in a stationary position. Then men called stock runners would get parts and bring them to the mechanics who were

Henry Ford (1863-1947)

This is the way cars looked in the "old days." An early result of mass production in auto-making was Ford's Model T. The first Model T was sold in 1908, but mass production of it did not come until 1913 when Henry Ford devised the assembly line. The model was discontinued in mid-1927 after almost 15½ million of them were manufactured.

building the automobile. Men would scurry back and forth like ants around an ant hill, and after many hours of work the mechanics would finally succeed in putting the car together.

Henry Ford was a mechanical genuis, and he knew that this system was too slow and costly. Besides, he had an ambition that could never be realized by this method of building cars. "I want to build a motor car for the great multitude," he said. "It will be so low in price that no man will be unable to own one."

Ford and his engineers knew that the first step to mass-produce cars was to manufacture parts in large numbers. The principle of making parts in quantity had been introduced by Eli Whitney, the inventor of the cotton gin, when he was making guns for the United States Army in 1798. Instead of making each gun by hand, Whitney built machines that made identical gun parts, one after another. These parts could then be quickly assembled into a finished gun.

Ford followed this practice by first inventing machines that would make identical automobile parts and make them fast. Parts were manufactured so carefully, and to such exact measurements, that each part was interchangeable with every other one like it.

The second step was to break away from the idea of building a car in a stationary position. The plan of bringing the work to the men, instead of the men to the work, had been originated by Oliver Evans in 1783 when he used conveyors in his grain mill. Only two men were needed to run the mill. One poured grain into a hopper at one end, while the other took flour off the other end. In between, everything was carried by conveyors.

The beginnings of a Model T car moves down the final assembly line in 1914 at Ford's Highland Park plant. Workers are installing the engine. Note the tracks in which the wheels were placed as the car was pushed along.

Henry Ford decided this idea could be used in making cars by moving the chassis of the automobile along a straight line, while workers stood along the line adding parts as it went by. This way, he thought, would be faster and many hours of time wasted by the stock runners going back and forth would be saved.

It was the summer of 1913. The Ford Motor

Company was making cars at a plant in Highland Park, a suburb of Detroit. One day Henry Ford decided to try out his plan for a moving assembly line. He attached a rope to a chassis on wheels and had several strong men pull it slowly along the floor. Men stationed at intervals placed parts on the chassis as it passed, and when the car came to the end of the line it was ready to drive away!

This was the first crude final assembly line, but it was the beginning of mass production of automobiles.

This was the body drop in the old days. The body slid down a wooden ramp and was fastened to the chassis.

The Final Assembly
Line Today

Today's final assembly line is much improved, of course. It moves along automatically and is a marvel of our day. Everything is timed to the split second. As the car travels along, conveyors bring parts and groups of parts (called subassemblies) to the final line. These conveyors are called "feeder" lines, because they feed parts to the final line.

Along the final line, four hundred workmen are stationed. They are unskilled workers, but each has been trained to do a particular job and is master of that one operation. These workmen take the parts from the conveyor and install them on the car. Each part must not only fit, it must also be the right color. After all, it would look very strange to add red fenders to a blue car, wouldn't it?

If you walk down a final assembly line, you will see a car "born" right before your eyes. Piece by

This is what the final assembly line looks like just before production of a new model. It is stripped for action.

piece the car takes shape. At the end of the line a workman gets into the car and turns the ignition switch. The engine roars, and he drives it away.

The same assembly line loaded with Mustangs.

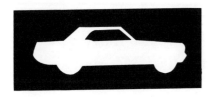

How The Mustang Was Assembled

Now let's get back to the Mustang. In early 1964, the Mustang was ready for production. All the preliminary work had been finished. The researchers had surveyed the market. The product planners had come up with a "paper plan." The designers had sketched the car and fashioned it in clay. The handmade prototypes had been made and tested.

The Stamping Plant had made the body panels and other sheet-metal parts. The Engine Plant had the engines ready. The Glass Plant had produced windows and windshields. The feeder lines were strung with parts. The final assembly line had been tooled up and staffed with capable workers. It was ready to move.

The time to assemble the first Mustang had come!

The first step in assembly of a car is building the body. This takes place on a feeder line that eventually winds its way to the final line.

The side panels, floor, and roof of the new Mustang were carefully fitted together. They were held in place by a viselike clamp called a framing fixture.

On the body feeder line, many joints must be welded by hand. This is called spot welding.

Workmen then welded the panels together. In the early days of car-making, pieces were secured with bolts and nuts. Welding is a big improvement, because it makes a stronger joint.

With the body panels fastened together, workmen then welded the body to the chassis. This was a new technique. For many years the chassis moved down the final line and the body was bolted to it. But the Mustang body and chassis were welded together before the body reached the final assembly line. This is called a unitized body.

After the Mustang body was unitized, the doors and trunk lid were put on. Then all the metal surfaces were ground smooth and cleaned.

Next came painting. First several primer coats were put on. Then the body was sanded and washed. Now it entered a spray booth, where men wearing protective masks applied two coats of final color. Finally the body moved along the conveyor into an oven, where the paint was baked hard.

Then the body, with its bright new colors, moved into the Trim Department. Trimming sounds simple, but it isn't. It means installing the instrument panel, steering column, windshields and windows, heater, radio, and all electrical wiring.

This is the paint spray booth where car bodies on the body line are given color before going on to the final assembly line.

Wiring an automobile so that all lights work is a difficult job. Headlamps, tail lights, the dome light, instrument panel lights, backup lights, glove-compartment lights—all must work. The job is simplified by the fact that skilled electricians share the wiring job. Each electrician takes a set of wires controlling certain lights and installs them separately. They scramble in and out of the body shell of the car as they do their work.

Once the interior trimming of the new Mustang was completed, the heart of the car—the engine—was added to the body shell and bolted in place.

In the meantime, on another feeder line, the front end of the Mustang was prepared. The front end included the front fenders, grille, radiator, and headlamps. This assembly was put through the same welding and painting process as the body. Both the body and the front end then moved along the feeder lines to the final assembly line, where they would be installed.

As the body, front end, other parts, and sub-assemblies started to move into place, the rear axle (the only part of the chassis still to be installed) began to move down the final line. Along both sides of the line, workmen waited for the axle and the body

These men are assembling engines. The engines hang from overhead conveyors so that the men can move them around with ease.

to come together. From that point, the car would travel 1,200 feet down the final assembly line and would emerge as a fine-looking Mustang.

Before the first Mustang was assembled, no man on the line had seen the complete car. Everyone was excited about building the new Mustang, but no one knew exactly what the car would look like when it was finished. Not until the body was attached would they have an idea just what the car was to look like.

Finally the dramatic moment came. Slowly the rear axle moved into place. High above, held in

One of the most dramatic moments on the final assembly line—the body drop. The body of a Mustang hangs high over a chassis, ready to drop down.

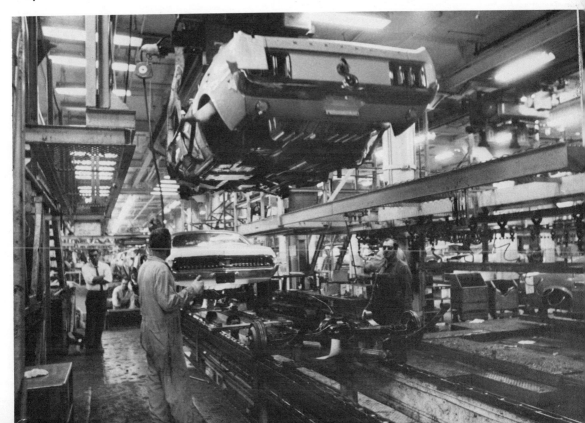

giant prongs, hung the first Mustang body. Slowly it was lowered until it fit snugly on the axle. Workers moved in to bolt it securely.

The men stared at the half-built car, and many of them smiled.

"It looks cool," one of the men on the line said.

Bit by bit, the car was fashioned. The carpeting was put in. Then the front end was attached. Now

When the first Mustangs came down the line, fenders were installed separately. The man on the right is installing a fender as the car moves down the final assembly line. Today, the fenders and grille are all one and are installed in one operation.

The hood, swinging down from a conveyor, is guided toward a slowly-moving Mustang by a workman.

the workers could really see the sporty lines of the Mustang. There were more smiles from men who felt that they had created this car with their hands.

"I'm going to buy one of these," another man said.

The enthusiasm that had gripped Ford officials when the new Mustang was just a dream had now

A workman is installing the front bumper and is tightening it with a power wrench. This takes place on the final line just before the wheels go on.

been transferred to the men who were actually putting the car together.

Now workmen began to add the finishing touches. The wheels were put on, the upholstered seats placed

Wheels are installed on the final line with magical quickness. The tool operated by this workman tightens all the wheel nuts at one time.

After the cars come off the final assembly line, inspectors check them over carefully for any "bugs" before they are shipped to dealers.

inside, accessories added—all fed to the men on feeder lines. Finally one man put six gallons of gasoline in the tank.

The new car was finished! A workman started the engine and drove the first Mustang off the line!

The date was March 9, 1964. The deadline had been met.

It had taken 17.1 hours to assemble the car, starting with the building of the body and front end on the feeder lines and ending with the finished automobile. The trip down the final assembly line itself had taken only fifty-two minutes. But after that first Mustang was completed, so many more were bunched behind that a new car rolled off the final assembly line *every sixty seconds!*

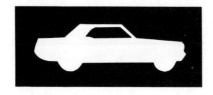

After The Assembly Line

Manufacturing the car isn't the end of the story. The next step is to make sure that people know about the car. This is known as promoting the car.

Ford Motor Company went all-out to promote its new car. The Mustang was introduced to newspaper and magazine reporters at the New York World's Fair. Advertising commercials on three major television networks reached twenty-nine million viewers. Newspaper and magazine ads appeared.

Meanwhile, Mustang cars were being shipped by train to cities throughout the United States. Then they were delivered to dealers by haul-away trucks.

The Mustang is introduced to crowds attending the World's Fair in New York City.

And on April 17, when the new car was officially introduced by Ford dealers, people crowded the showroom floors.

But just filling a need for a product is not enough. There is a great deal of competition in the automobile industry, as well as in other industries. Soon other manufacturers, fighting to stay in competition, also produced this type of car.

Haul-away trucks like this one deliver cars to dealers all across the country.

However, all automobile companies must make changes in their cars from year to year, if they want to stay in business. They do this in two ways: by continuously improving the cars they build, and by introducing new models.

One recent improvement in automobiles has been in the field of pollution. Car makers have taken steps to reduce exhaust fumes, and much progress has already been made. For example, Ford's 1972 models (including Mustangs) are equipped with some emission controls. Work is continuing on this problem throughout the car industry.

As for introducing new models, a few months after the Mustang appeared, Ford added a model called a fastback to the Mustang line. In 1970, two more Mustangs—the Mach 1 and the Grandé—were added.

Today, to keep up with the demands of car buyers, automobile manufacturers offer them many choices. So as you travel the nation's highways, look about you at some of the millions of cars. Like the Mustang, each type was probably one man's dream which had its beginnings at the drawing board.

Some of the millions of cars on today's high-speed superhighways.

110